CHAKRAS

A Thorough Manual Of Self Healing Methods, Balance Your Energy For Wellness & Transformation

(Your Definitive Manual For Using Healing To Reach Your Higher Self)

Abelino Vicente

TABLE OF CONTENT

Healing Affirmations For The Work Done In The Shadow 1

How To Awaken Kundalini Energy Through The Root Chakra 4

The Svadhishthana Chakra Is The Second Of The Seven Chakras 14

The Upper Chakras, Including The Major And Minor Chakras 26

Getting Your Bearings Through Mantra 30

Healing And Balancing The Solar Plexus Chakra Can Be Accomplished Through The Following Practices: 37

Increase The Flow Of Shakti By Practicing Several Types Of Guided Meditation 43

What Are The Roots Of A Chakra Blockage In The Throat? 47

An Explanation Of The Third Eye Chakra From A Scientific Perspective 59

Acquiring Knowledge Of The Body's Various Energy Centers 64

The Navataras: An Explanation Of Their Meanings 72

Recognizing And Appreciating One's Physical Form Through Self-Love, Self-Care, And Body Positivity 84

The Strength Of One's Own Suggestions 88

The Law Of Cause And Effect Is Associated With The Root Chakra- Karma...95

Developing A Sacred Environment......................99

Awareness Of The Heart Chakra Through The Use Of Crystals And Essential Oils 105

The First Chakras, Also Known As The Root Chakras 114

Healing Through Chakras And How It Affects Relationships... 126

The Chakra Of Verbal Expression..................... 133

Cat And Cow Pose, Also Known As Marjaryasana-Bitilasana 148

Find Ways To Disconnect From Society And Reconnect With Yourself, And Good Luck With That! 162

After Having Gathered Your Energy In The Belly, You Will Now Send It To Various Chakra Areas. 167

Healing Affirmations For The Work Done In The Shadow

Affirmations are known to have a significant impact on the healing process. The use of generic affirmations can be helpful in kicking off the healing process, despite the fact that they are frequently put to use in order to address particular problems. The following are some sentences that will be of assistance to you as you embark on this journey:

I open myself up to healing, and I forge ahead with strength.

My shortcomings are not indicative of my value or of who I am.

I adore and accept every facet of who I am with every fiber of my being.

I treasure the person that I am maturing into.

I am making progress in my recovery from the traumas of the past.

I let go of any feelings of guilt or shame, and I forgive myself for all the decisions I've made in the past.

I love and respect my parents despite the fact that they are who they are.

I am willing to accept responsibility for my deeds and grow as a result of my blunders.

The traumatic event that I have been through is not my fault, and I release any self-blame that I may have had.

I use the difficult experiences of my past to inform my decision-making for the future and help ensure its success.

I cannot be held accountable for the things that occurred to me when I was a child.

I have made the decision to let go of old grievances and to be forgiving toward everyone in my life.

The only validation and respect I require is that which I give myself, and I honor and respect myself.

My history of traumatic experiences does not give me the right to inflict pain on other people, and I am dedicated to improving myself and maturing as a human being.

I don't deserve to be in depleting or toxic relationships or experiences; I deserve relationships and experiences that boost me up and help me grow.

I am aware of the errors I have made in the past and will make every effort to develop and progress in the years to come.

I have made the decision to forgive because I believe it will offer me peace and free me from the responsibilities of holding resentment.

Confronting my feelings helps me become more self-aware and strengthens the resolve I already possess.

I am appreciative of the process of maturing and getting better, and I am thankful for every aspect of who I am.

I am maturing and making peace with my past, and as a result, I am both stronger and better than I was in the past.

You are free to include these affirmations into your daily Shadow work practice by repeating them with conviction and letting the positive energy emanating from them to infiltrate every aspect of your being.

How To Awaken Kundalini Energy Through The Root Chakra

When activated, the potent feminine energy of the kundalini, which is located in the root chakra, will cause your consciousness to expand. The more time you spend in nature, the more you will be able to access the kundalini energy that is located at the base of your spine. This access will increase as you release blockages from your root chakra and become more grounded. An awakening of the kundalini is a phenomenon that can be triggered by practices such as meditation, yoga, dance, and grounding. The process of letting this kundalini energy flow out of the base of the spine and into the rest of the body may be very therapeutic, reassuring, and empowering. Awakenings of the Kundalini are practiced in modern times as a technique of effecting personal development and gaining empowerment. It will bring about beneficial changes in your life that are lasting and lasting. The following is how kundalini awakenings typically feel:

You will feel large, expansive, and at ease as you enter a deep level of ecstasy. You will feel as though you are entering another dimension.

You will feel like you belong here on earth and that your divine presence is an ecstatic and purposeful one. You will experience being more in touch with your psychic abilities and spiritual gifts. Your level of creativity will also expand. You will be inspired to make more meaningful changes in your life. Your positivity will spread to those around you. A natural state of joy and freedom will fill up your senses. You will have more compassion, joy, and empathy for others. You

In Chapter 3, you will get additional knowledge regarding the practice of kundalini yoga as a means of releasing blockages in your root chakra.

Additional Methods for Releasing Blockages in Your Root Chakra

In order to open your root chakra, you can use essential oils such as frankincense, grapefruit, and vetiver. Your entire disposition will change, and you will feel rejuvenated with a bigger level of optimism. Open your heart to abundance, and begin taking steps in your life that will lead to more positive results, which will get rid of the fear that you have to survive. You can also follow along with guided meditations on abundance that are found online and make a commitment to living a life filled with endless possibilities. You can begin your practice of bountiful meditation by looking for examples of it on YouTube.

● The energetic shift in your root chakra will be stronger along with the degree to which you are able to transform by distancing and expanding the scope of your thoughts from your phobias. To open the root chakra, practice positive affirmations such as the following: "I am safe. " "I am grounded." "I am abundant." "The Earth supports and nourishes me." "I am enough." "I have nothing to fear." "I am enough." Utilize the color red in your work. Consume foods that are red in color, such as grapefruit, red peppers, and strawberries. Take risks, and elevate your energetic frequency to one of self-assurance by surrounding yourself with vibrant reds.

During your meditations, it is beneficial to make use of red crystals like garnet, red jasper, hematite, red calcite, and obsidian. While you meditate and bring your attention to the color red, you can place these crystals in the palm of your hand.

Feel what emotions need to be released from this chakra in order to make it strong and in balance again, and then visualize a red light running throughout your entire body from your root chakra. This light will help you feel what emotions need to be released. To begin, recite the Sanskrit word "lam."

While you're outside in the natural world, try to get more in touch with your roots. Walk about barefoot on the grass while visualizing a beam of red light emanating from the base of your spine and traveling all the way down to the ground. As you move forward in this direction, let go of any anxiety or negativity that may be holding you back.

● You may also choose to engage in some gardening. While you are outside, choose a comfortable spot to sit on the grass, rest one hand on your heart and the other hand on the ground, and exhale slowly and deeply many times. Attempt to maintain this position for a minimum of ten breaths (Unblocking Your Sacral Chakra for Confidence and Creativity, 2022).

Both religious and secular forms of meditation place a significant emphasis on the practice of mindfulness as an essential component. The secular approach to stress reduction known as mindfulness-based stress reduction was created by Jon Kabat-Zinn and his team, and it has gained widespread recognition in many parts of the world. This path's initial and primary objective was to provide assistance to patients in a medical setting, such as in the case of chronic pain; nevertheless, its benefits for maintaining our overall health and happiness were quickly recognized, and "MBSR" courses have since proliferated all over the world. The initial and primary objective of this path was to provide assistance to patients in a medical setting.

Through the cultivation of mindfulness, we are able to root ourselves firmly in the here and now. You can practice with the following sankalpa (see Chamber 4) to help you become more mindful not only during meditation sessions, but also in your day-to-day life: "I am always mindful and fully present."

Repeat this both before and after your meditation sessions, and don't forget to check in with yourself often during the day to remind yourself to re-root yourself by being attentive of who you are, where you are, and the things that are happening in your life.

It is not necessary to concentrate on just one item in order to engage in mindful practice. Being attentive involves paying attention to what we are actually witnessing in the now and not allowing our attention to wander from one moment to the next. Mindfulness can also refer to the practice of reflecting on our internal and external sensory experiences as well as the act of constructing ideas.

Remove yourself from the context.

It is highly likely that you are reading this material while holding a book in your hand. If you purchased it as an electronic book, you can perform the exercise on either a tablet or a computer; nonetheless, it is still valid.

If you are seated in a chair, position your feet so that they form a straight angle with the floor underneath them. Adjust your posture so that your spine is in a straight line.

Your hips, abdomen, shoulders, and jaw should all be relaxed while you maintain an upright stance.

Now take a look at the reading material you have. You might be able to move it so that it is just in front of your eyes, or you might be able to position it so that it is far enough in front of you that you can maintain an upright posture while gazing at it.

Take some time to reflect on the words that you are currently reading. What are they trying to say? How do they appear to you? I was wondering what language you were reading the book in.

Next, take a look at the thing, the medium, on which these words are written or printed for you to read. You should make an effort to pay attention to the diverse colors, the different forms of the letters, and the various textures of the materials that were used to construct this book or reader. If you stare closely enough at a screen, you might be able to make out the individual pixels.

Are you able, if only for a short while, to set aside your knowledge, to ignore the meaning of these words, and to concentrate instead on what is materially there, now, and here?

Continue doing this for approximately one more minute, and then go back to reading the text consciously.

The Svadhishthana Chakra Is The Second Of The Seven Chakras.

This chakra is related with the conquest of water and can be found slightly above the Muladhara at the base of the penis or in the center of the lower back. Its emblems include the crescent and the God Vishnu, who nourishes the principle of the universe. Its color is typically described as crimson or red, however white can also be used to describe it. The power of this chakra is carried by Ragini Shakti, a dark blue goddess with three red eyes and four hands, who is seated on a lotus flower and whose blood pours from her nose. She is pictured here with a chisel, a drum, a trident, and a lotus flower in her hands. An animal that resembles a crocodile and is either light gray or green in color is considered to be a symbol of the chakra. This creature personifies dominion over the ocean and indicates a link with one's unconscious. A person can triumph over the forces of nature by focusing on this chakra.

She has six petals, which stand for the mental traits of neglect, numbness, credulity, suspicion, desire for destruction, and cruelty. She also has six nerves that are connected to the colon, rectum, kidneys, bladder, genitals, and testicles, among other organs and parts of the body. This chakra is thought to be the core of a person's heterosexual orientation, and it is responsible for promoting the circulation of liquid fluids throughout the body, as well as their preservation and sustenance.

According to Mishra, this chakra is responsible for the regulation, maintenance, and nourishment of the foot. By concentrating on it, a person feels a magnetic pulsation, circulation, and vibration in his legs, and they are able to rid themselves of any unpleasant feelings, pains, or illnesses that they are experiencing in those areas. Problems with sexuality, diabetes, and illnesses affecting the kidneys and bladder are some of the other disorders linked to this chakra. By meditating on one's ego, one can free themselves from egocentric feelings as well as minute impulses and cravings. The mental fortitude and calmness that one possesses grows. The regular functioning of the Svadhishthana is related with a feeling of self-confidence and overall well-being, as well as the difficulties that she experiences in her career, disappointment, addiction, and anxiety. This chakra is also connected to one's sense of taste as well as their ability to communicate verbally. Tantras teach that in order to become proficient in it, one must first become fluent in the language of it.

Manipura Chakra, also known as the Third Chakra

Manipura, which is located above Svadvishthana and opposite the navel, is connected with the god Rudra, who is said to be responsible for the distribution of things as well as the creation of fear. He personifies the destructive force of the universe, which is the realm of the mind. One of the texts explains how the goddess Lakini Shakti, who is depicted wearing yellow garments and is known as the benefactress of the universe, enjoys eating animal meat, has blood pouring down her chest, and has fat dripping from her lips. She is dubbed the benefactress of the cosmos. The ram, which is an animal that is commonly slaughtered, serves as the animal symbol because it personifies the need to sacrifice addictions, impulsive drives, and other powerful emotions.

When one focuses their attention on the Manipura chakra, they gain an understanding of excrement or of time itself. It's possible that this level of openness can be linked to the recalling of memories from previous lifetimes or states that carry people beyond the limits of consciousness that are imposed by the passage of time. This chakra is also associated with the regulation of heat and is responsible for directing Agni, the principle of fire, which is responsible for regulating the creature's unrestrained movements and digestive system. In particular, the function of the stomach, liver, and large intestine is governed by Manipura, which is related with a portion of the central nervous system that is situated above the lumbar area. Manipura also supervises the internal organs of the abdominal cavity. Some people believe that by meditating on the color red and concentrating on this area, it is possible to heal disorders that affect the abdominal organs.

This chakra is made up of ten petals, each of which is associated with one of the following emotions: humiliation, betrayal, envy, desire, drowsiness, despair, vainness, delusion, disgust, and fear. On the other hand, one of the tantric books claims that when a yogi meditates on this chakra and pronounces a mul mantra, he is never in a bad mood, and sicknesses are unable to enter their body. This type of yogi is able to enter the bodies of other people and view Siddhas, which are holy men and women who teach yoga. They are also able to detect at a glance the characteristics of material objects and see things that are buried underground. It should come as no surprise that this chakra is linked so frequently with attaining power and establishing one's rightful place in the world. It is particularly difficult because the emphasis is placed on various Zen meditations. The opening of this chakra involves the participation of the eyes and such control over their movements so that they do not, even for a moment, come off the center between the eyebrows. This concentration gives rise to a sense of stability and robustness in the being.

Sapphire is known to aid in the enhancement of mental clarity, the promotion of spiritual growth, and the bringing of mental, physical, and spiritual equilibrium and harmony.

The corundum mineral family includes the valuable gemstone known as sapphire. It is one of the minerals that has the highest hardness rating. It is widely regarded for the deep, rich blue hue that is devoid of any inclusions, which gives it its distinctive appearance.

This is due to the fact that the center of the earth is an extremely hot and pressurized environment where sapphire is formed. In addition to this, its hue might vary greatly based on the trace elements that were present during the time when it was being made.

It is known as a stone of knowledge and mental clarity, and it is believed that using it can boost a person's psychic and intuitive abilities. It was believed to provide defense against potentially dangerous elements. One more thing that's been said about sapphire is that it has a soothing, tranquil energy that can assist alleviate anxiety and tension, in addition to fostering emotions of calm and peace.

The throat chakra is linked to sapphire and is responsible for expression and communication. Sapphire is associated with the throat chakra. It is said that it can assist one in telling the truth and in expressing oneself clearly and strongly. In addition to this, it is said that wearing a sapphire can help one achieve enlightenment and a higher level of spiritual consciousness. It is said to enhance one's capacity for self-expression, stimulate creativity, and improve one's ability to communicate.

REAL PROPERTY

The most common hue for a sapphire is a dark blue, although other colors, such as pink, yellow, green, orange, and even purple, can also be found inside a sapphire.

On the Mohs scale of mineral hardness, sapphire comes in at a ranking of 9, which indicates that it is a highly hard and long-lasting gemstone.

Clarity: Sapphire has excellent clarity, and high-quality stones have very few, if any, visible inclusions that may be seen in the stone. They are available in a wide variety of clarity grades, ranging from completely eye-clean to quite densely included.

Sapphire is thought to assist improve mental clarity, encourage spiritual growth, and provide balance and harmony to the mind, body, and spirit. Its spiritual attributes can be found in the gemstone sapphire.

Gemstone varieties: Blue Sapphire, Pink Sapphire, Yellow Sapphire, Green Sapphire, White Sapphire, Purple Sapphire, Black Sapphire, Orange Sapphire, Bi-color Sapphire, Star Sapphire, Color-Change Sapphire, Parti Sapphire, Montana Sapphire, Starry Sapphire, Cornflower Blue Sapphire, Lavender Sapphire, Peach Sapphire, Teal Sapphire, Champagne Sapphire, Padparadscha Sapphire.

The countries of Sri Lanka, Madagascar, Tanzania, Australia, and the United States are all good places to look for sapphires.

The Upper Chakras, Including The Major And Minor Chakras

Our vital life force energy permeates the entire body and resounds from the head to the toes. This energy moves through the seven primary chakras, each of which corresponds to a particular component of our bodily, mental, emotional, and spiritual experience. In Sanskrit, the names for these seven chakras are as follows: Muladhara (Root), Svadhisthana (Sacral), Manipura (Solar Plexus), Anahata (Heart), Vishuddha (Throat), Ajna (Third Eye), and Sahasrara (Crown).

The three lower chakras—the Root, Sacral, and Solar Plexus—keep us connected to the material world and are responsible for maintaining our sense of survival, creativity, and power. The three chakras located at the top of the body are known as the spiritual chakras. These chakras are associated with our ability to express ourselves, our intuition, and our connection to the divine. The physical world and the spiritual realm meet in the center at the Heart Chakra, also known as the heart of love. Each of the seven chakras can be found along the central channel, also known as the Sushumnanadi, which travels through the spine. In traditional Chinese medicine (TCM), the meridians and nadis are the pathways via which energy travels from one chakra to another. Nadis are similar to these meridians.

Each chakra has an effect on both our mental and emotional states. They are associated with a variety of sensations, thoughts, and beliefs that play a role in the development of our personalities and behaviors. For instance, the Sacral

Chakra is linked to experiences like euphoria, pleasure, and originality in one's work. When this chakra is out of alignment, we may experience feelings of depression or guilt, in addition to a blockage in our creative abilities.

Additionally, they have an effect on the workings of our bodies on the inside. They are linked to a variety of organs, glands, and systems that have an impact on our general well-being. As an illustration, the adrenal glands, bones, and legs are all associated with the Root Chakra. We may experience difficulties such as weariness, lower back discomfort, or constipation when this chakra is out of balance in our bodies.

In order to heal the chakras properly, it is necessary to have a solid understanding of what each chakra actually stands for at its most fundamental level. What is its primary function, and how should the chakra look in order for it to be healthy? How may I get in touch with them through the usage of associations, such as a certain color or symbol? What sage advice would they like for me to take to heart? As soon as we have an understanding of the fundamental nature of each chakra, we will be able to feel it, heal it, and control it.

Getting Your Bearings Through Mantra

The use of mantras as a form of meditation is one practice that can assist you in transporting this energy with you wherever you go. With this method, one repeats a word or sentence over and over again until the straightforward expression of the idea becomes connected to and aligned with the person's energy and vibration. In this scenario, you could create a mantra that relates to the tree (which represents you), the branches (which represent your mind), the trunk and the bark (which represent your body and skin), the wind and the rain (which represent your thoughts, emotions, and distractions), the roots (which represent your root chakra and your grounding cord), and the base that connects all of us (the earth).

Meditation Guide Number Two

Step 1

For the time being, let us construct a mantra. How about this one for starters: "I am strong and sturdy, like a tree that has stood the test of time." I establish my roots in the soil and am firmly rooted in the earth by way of my very own center and my very own base. Just like a tree, I mature and produce new offspring. My roots are vast and unending, much like the roots of the tree. I am the stillness that lasts forever. I am that which develops." Recite the phrase with me once more: "I am sturdy and strong, like a tree that has stood the test of time." I establish my roots in the soil and am firmly rooted in the earth by way of my very own center and my very own base. Just like a tree, I mature and produce new offspring. My roots are vast and unending, much like the roots of the tree. I am the stillness that lasts forever. I am that which develops." If you find that the length of this mantra is too much for you, you can take one sentence from what I've just spoken - the statement that stood out to you the most – and repeat just that phrase instead.

Step 2: While you are repeating this mantra again and over, keep in mind everything you saw in the previous step with the tree, its roots, and its branches. Also, keep in mind how all of this ties to your own body and the experiences you will have in the future. Be like a tree: steadfast, solid, self-assured, robust, towering, and inspired with each subsequent repeat. Get in touch with your roots through feeling connected to the soil. Feel yourself become more receptive to the possibilities that exist as the mantra is distilled into a single, pure, vibrating, and energetic representation of optimism. Allow the energy of your root chakra to flow freely as you go deeper within yourself and establish a home both there and on the earth.

The fifth chakra of the body

I am delighted to guide you through a fantastic meditation for the throat chakra. Permit me to walk you through the process of unlocking and balancing the fifth Chakra, which is the one that sets your inner voice free and provides you with the ultimate truth in what you say. It is the place where you produce and manifest the words that influence the world that is all around you, and it is the center of speech. Get yourself into one of your favorite spots so that you can forget about the rest of the world and relax. Making sure that you are in a position that is comfortable for you. Relax by taking a deep breath in and then letting it out slowly. When you are meditating on the chakras and putting your mind on each one in turn, you can choose at any time to close your eyes. This allows you to more effectively balance the chakras. You start to recognize that the occurrences in your life are symbolic, and that there are valuable lessons to be gained from them. Take a deep breath in and then slowly exhale it. Relax each inhale and exhale completely. You focus all of your attention on the throat chakra by repeating the action of breathing in and out again. Now it is located smack dab in the middle of your throat, and it is depicted by a lovely, clear blue that is comparable to the color of the sky or the ocean. Imagine this Chakra as an eight-sided mandala with elaborate motifs filling it. This is one way to help you visualize it. Feel the power of your imagination as it gives you the ability to turn this chakra.

It is becoming quicker and faster until you realize that it is moving more quickly than anything else you have ever seen. This mantra should be repeated five times. My words are particularly without guile. My words are particularly without guile. My words are particularly without guile. My words are particularly without guile. My words are particularly without guile. Take a long, deep breath in through your nose, and while you do so, allow the breath to enlarge the throat chakra such that it is radiating outward in all directions from your body. Nice. Experience the strength of your words' ability to connect with others. In all sincerity, how would you characterize the sensation that is associated with the throat chakra? It involves opening your throat up to such a degree that it is completely free and broad, so enabling the truth to flow freely out of you. The sensation that you have in your throat adds a touch of affection to what you say. You are able to see the throat chakra completely open and unrestricted, and you can feel it spinning with a magnificent blue light that is comparable to the color of the sky. Good. Take a deep breath in, and while you do so, picture yourself drawing the power of the spirit into your throat so that it can influence the words that you speak. With a simplicity that you had long since forgotten till now. It is flowing gently down from here to your entire body, illuminating all of the other chakras along the way, and providing them with the energy to begin opening and moving in truth.

You are aware of the words, and I am speaking in all honesty. The throat chakra is now entirely open, and it is prepared to re-establish a connection between you and your genuine speech. Experiencing the honesty that you had forgotten was still within you as it came rushing out in a natural way. Take a long, deep breath for the very last time. Take a deep breath in and then let it out. That's wonderful. Make a conscious effort to bring your attention back to the here and now by focusing on the area around you. Stretch your body in whatever way that is comfortable for you, open your eyes, and get ready to use the power of your voice for the greater good.

Healing And Balancing The Solar Plexus Chakra Can Be Accomplished Through The Following Practices:

It is essential to engage in practices that develop and strengthen our personal power and self-esteem if we wish for the Solar Plexus Chakra to be healed and brought back into equilibrium. Consider some of the following strategies that have shown to be effective:

1. Cultivating Self-Awareness: Take the time to reflect on your accomplishments, as well as your values and the things that are important to you. You should be proud of all of your achievements, no matter how insignificant they may seem. This routine facilitates the growth of a more profound feeling of self-worth as well as confidence in one's own capabilities.

2. Establishing limits: It is important to learn how to establish limits in your relationships and interactions that are both obvious and healthy. Maintain a respectful attitude toward the personal space boundaries of others while using assertiveness in the expression of your own wants and aspirations. This contributes to the enhancement of your own power as well as the establishment of a sense of equilibrium and respect in the context of your contacts.

Engage in physical activities that activate and build the core muscles, such as yoga postures like Boat Pose (Navasana) or Pilates exercises. 3. Core-Activating Exercises: Engage in physical activities that activate and strengthen the core muscles. This assists in reawakening and energizing the Solar Plexus Chakra, which in turn promotes a sense of personal power and inner fortitude.

4. Reinforce Your Self-Esteem and Personal Power Through Visualization and Affirmations Make use of the power of visualization and affirmations to help you reinforce your sense of self-worth and personal power. You are going to want to close your eyes, imagine a blazing yellow light in your Solar Plexus Chakra, and then repeat positive affirmations to yourself like "I am worthy," "I am confident," or "I embrace my personal power." Please give yourself time to let these positive affirmations permeate your subconscious thinking.

5. Adopt an Empowering Mindset and Replace Negative Self-Talk with Positive Thoughts and words Pay attention to your internal dialogue and replace negative self-talk and self-doubt with positive thoughts and words. Put limiting beliefs to the test and rethink how you may use them in a constructive

and encouraging way. You have the ability to improve your sense of self-worth and acknowledge your personal power by adjusting your thinking.

6. Taking Action Based on Inspiring Ideas: Get out of your comfort zone and start taking inspired action to achieve the objectives and aspirations you've set for yourself. Begin with baby steps, then work your way up to more challenging activities as you get more comfortable. Your personal power will be bolstered and your Solar Plexus Chakra will be strengthened with every action you perform that is in harmony with your own self.

A person's inner fortitude, personal power, and self-confidence can be accessed through their Solar Plexus Chakra. We may unlock its transformational power and build a life filled with empowerment and self-assurance if we comprehend its role and significance, investigate its emotional and energy elements, and participate in therapeutic techniques.

It is important to keep in mind that the process of healing and balancing the Solar Plexus Chakra is an ongoing one that calls for self-awareness, self-care, and practices that are done on purpose. Recognize your own strength, value who you are, and have faith in your ability to make decisions that serve your best interests. You will radiate a magnetic energy that attracts opportunities and helps you in the process of manifesting your wishes if you establish a strong feeling of self-esteem and confidence as you work through this lesson.

As you continue your exploration of the chakras, it is important to keep in mind that each energy center is interrelated with and has an effect on the others. By focusing your attention on the Solar Plexus Chakra, you are not only able to boost your own power and sense of self-worth, but you are also able to clear the path for the waking and alignment of the other chakras. Embrace the process, have faith in what you're doing, and be grateful for the profound wisdom and transformation that lie ahead.

Increase The Flow Of Shakti By Practicing Several Types Of Guided Meditation.

Before they are able to concentrate adequately to visualize these subtle inner motions, a lot of people need assistance to detach themselves from the distractions that the mind and the outside world present. In circumstances such as these, I always advise practicing guided meditation. There are a lot of different strategies that people discuss on online meditation forums and even on websites like YouTube that can help you raise your kundalini. You can find these techniques everywhere online. The instruction you'll need to be able to turn off that conscious brain and simply, meditatively focus on the shakti - that pure and potent source of energy that wants to move within you – can also be provided via audio books of guided meditations. These can give you the ability to shut off that conscious brain. It will be to your great benefit to seek out these guided meditations for kundalini awakening.

You might try to bring the kundalini energy that is located at the crown of your head to the surface.

When compared to other techniques, this one emphasizes attention to detail a little bit more than most of the others do. It all comes down to how you imagine the kundalini energy traveling from the base of your spine all the way up to the peak of your head, and then descending again. In essence, you should experiment with shifting the focus of your attention. though you've been visualizing things (as most of us will inherently do), as though the serpent has been rising from your base – with that root chakra as your energetic core from which it leaves and to which it eventually returns - swap things up in a way that is both impactful and subtle. This will help you better understand how the serpent interacts with you. Imagine that your kundalini is being attracted up through your body as if it were being drawn by a magnet that is located in the crown of your head, and think of your crown chakra as being the energetic core of your body. Then, once the kundalini has risen to this crown point, picture yourself removing the "magnet" and allowing the snake to "fall" back down to the opposite end of its body before replacing the magnet. Keep in mind that although appearing human, you are actually a spiritual being having a human experience, as many people have stated in other places. Once you have reclaimed your crown chakra as your "source" of energy, shakti energy will respond favorably to the fact that it houses your most unadulterated potential.

What Are The Roots Of A Chakra Blockage In The Throat?

There is a wide variety of possible explanations for why your throat chakra is obstructed. In general, those that originate in the lower chakra are the most prevalent. Your body is receptive to the natural lifeforce when it enters at your root chakra, and because all of your chakras are related to one another, the energy has to work its way up to the higher levels. Now, if the lower chakras are blocked, they won't let the energy flow towards the throat chakra, which will throw it out of balance. This is because the lower chakras are connected to the higher chakras. In a similar manner, if they are overactive, they will deliver a surge of energy that your throat chakra is unable to process, which will cause it to become overworked.

Upper respiratory infections, hyper or hypothyroidism, and other physical problems can be both the cause of and a symptom of a dysfunction in the vishuddha. Because these disorders frequently give the appearance of being secondary to other medical issues, people frequently confuse them with those other conditions. If they go untreated for an extended period of time, they will start to impact the center of the throat, causing it to hurt physically, mentally, and emotionally.

The throat chakra can become blocked for a variety of reasons, including emotional and mental disorders, which can have their roots in a number of different places. Trauma to the body can lead to trauma to the mind, which can make it difficult for you to communicate your pain and other negative feelings. It is also possible for one to experience emotional stress in the absence of any physical symptoms. For example, you may have experienced a traumatic emotional experience but feel too ashamed to discuss it with others. Hiding your pain will make you feel nervous or sad, both of which can be harmful to your immune system and can lead to a wide range of health symptoms. If you try to hide your suffering, you will feel anxious or depressed.

Even if energy would ordinarily flow via your throat chakra, it is possible for it to go dormant due to inertia if you are pressured to suppress your desires and remain loyal to who you are for an extended period of time. This tendency is frequently observed in victims of verbal and emotional abuse as well as victims of gaslighting.

What Can You Find Inside a Chakra?

In contemporary Western culture, there has been a lot of debate concerning the impact that one's physical appearance plays in their mental health. Many of our experiences, both positive and negative, can be kept in the organs and nervous system of the body, as is detailed in books such as "The Body Keeps the Score" (2014) written by Bessel van der Kolk. You can even observe this happening in real time with the bodily symptoms of anxiety or the physical triggers that are related with trauma. According to the theory and practice of chakras, the body does really keep track of the score. Chakra healers have argued for millennia that chakras not only store energy centers but also fundamental parts of our lives, both mentally and physically. This belief dates back to ancient India. Your chakras have the ability to record your experiences, including your memories, habits, and experiences. They not only have a sharp recall but also play a role in the formation of our identities. On the other hand, as you are undoubtedly already aware, the characteristics that help define who you are can also act as a barrier to your success. It is essential to build a more full understanding of yourself and where you have come from in order to form a more complete understanding of your chakras and what they are keeping within of them.

Chakras have the ability to hold not just the past but also the present and the future as well. What your future self or life will be like is determined by the state that your chakras are in at this now. In addition to this, your hopes, ambitions, and thoughts on the future are stored within your chakras. This is illustrated more physically in the higher chakras, which are concerned with planning and the future, as well as in the lower chakras, which are concerned with the individual's identity and sense of self-worth. Your views about yourself and your destiny are stored deep inside your chakras, which means that your chakras have a significant influence on your future in the form of the beliefs you have about yourself and your future. As a result, with the help of this new factor, we are able to understand how the energy of the chakras freely travels between the body and the outside world. In the same way that your ideas and experiences have an effect on your chakras, your chakras will also have an effect on the experiences you have in the future. Because of this, it is clear that the body is responsible for creating reality, just as reality is responsible for creating the body. Put this information to use so that you might experience a deeper sense of connectedness to the world around you.

Developing an Effective Plan for Physical Activity

Never let a lack of time or any other fictitious barrier prevent you from engaging in physical activity as a means of relieving stress or despair. The following advice will assist you in putting together an exercise routine that you will be able to maintain.

• Get your morning start on time by rising early. It affords you additional time.

• Start your workout as soon as you get out of bed.

Start your day off well by getting some exercise. You'll have a sense of self-efficacy and boundless energy for the rest of the day. The motivation you get from the realization that you have already completed one significant item on your to-do list allows you to be even more productive in the hours that follow.

- Maintain brevity, intensity, and coherence throughout.

It is more vital to perform short intensive workouts on a consistent basis as opposed to long workouts that are performed with ease here and then.

- Enlist the help of a training partner.

If you know that your workout partner anticipates your presence at the gym or at the start of your morning jog, you are more likely to keep your commitment to go.

- Figure out when you have the most free time to work out.

Avoid going to the gym at the same time every other person does. When you want to save time, avoid the rush hours.

- Schedule your workouts for off-hours.

There is no such thing as the "right" time to work out. Keep an open mind about the potential of working out at unorthodox times, especially if your duties, circumstances, and job schedule make it possible. People who choose to exercise when everyone else is asleep can take advantage of the fact that some gyms are open round-the-clock to meet their needs.

· Try not to overextend yourself.

People who overdo their workout routine are more likely to quit, particularly when they are just starting out. Take care not to injure yourself or tire yourself out. Begin on a low scale. Increase the amount of effort you put into your program once you have become accustomed to it. Gradually work your way up to it.

- Do not make the justification that you will get too tired to engage in other activities.

In the first few weeks of beginning a new fitness routine, it is common for those who have never exercised before to experience symptoms such as fatigue and soreness. However, as you grow adjusted to your program, you will notice that your workouts are making you stronger and giving you more energy. This is a direct result of your efforts. Exercising provides you with more energy. It contributes to your increased level of productivity.

- Don't believe the myth that you can only workout in a gym setting.

Going to the gym regularly offers a number of beneficial effects. On the other hand, you can reap the same benefits from exercising at home as you do from doing it in a gym setting. If you are short on time and resources, it is best to complete your workout program at home. It is quite acceptable to simply go for a fast walk or run instead. If you choose to act in a way that is simple and uncomplicated, you will inevitably find that you continue to behave in this manner throughout the course of time.

•Make going to the gym a daily routine.

When physical activity is a regular part of your routine, you won't even have to think about doing it. Putting on your workout clothes and being done with it is all that is required of you. You just have to force yourself to complete the task, even if you don't feel like it.

• Give a variety of physical activities a shot to see which ones you enjoy doing the most.

Exerting yourself physically in any way helps alleviate depression. You can choose from a wide variety of activities, such as team sports, individual sports, running, jogging, strength training, yoga, flexibility training, and many more activities. As long as you maintain a steady routine, you will be able to improve your mental health.

An Explanation Of The Third Eye Chakra From A Scientific Perspective

It's no exaggeration to say that the third eye chakra is a profoundly spiritual idea. Nevertheless, in recent years there has been a rise in the number of people interested in the scientific workings of this chakra. Despite the fact that many experts continue to be skeptical of this idea, there are some who are interested in gaining a scientific knowledge of what the "third eye" is and how it works. The pineal gland, the hypothalamus, and the pituitary gland are the areas of the brain that have been linked to the concept of a third eye. These are typically related with a person's mental health, vision, the quality of sleep they get, and their spiritual consciousness.

The Gland of the Pineal

In the area of the brain known as the epithalamus, an endocrine gland known as the pineal gland can be found. This gland, which is about the size of a pea and shaped like a pinecone, is responsible for regulating our circadian cycles by producing and controlling the levels of melatonin in the body. This gland collaborates with a section of the hypothalamus to keep track of the amount of light that each of our eyes is exposed to at any one time.

Melatonin is a hormone that is produced in proportion to the amount of darkness that our eyes are exposed to. To put it another way, melatonin is produced by our bodies while we are asleep at night. Because of the reduction in melatonin production that occurs throughout the day, we are more awake and alert. There is an internal clock in each and every one of us, and it operates in accordance with our circadian cycles. Our circadian rhythms are considered to be healthy when our sleep and wake cycles are regular. This not only guarantees that we have good bodily and mental health, but it also keeps us from letting anxiety and stress take control of our life. Our internal circadian rhythms become disrupted whenever we don't get enough or the right kind of sleep or when we sleep at the wrong time. This not only makes us feel more exhausted than usual, but it also has the potential to alter our moods and levels of energy in a more long-term manner over the course of time.

In addition to being responsible for controlling our sleep-wake cycles, the pineal gland is also involved in the maintenance of our reproductive and sexual health, as well as our immune system and the way we age. The third eye, also known as the pineal gland, has a significant influence on our bodies and our states of physical and mental health. For instance, having normal levels of melatonin and maintaining a regular sleep-wake cycle can have an effect on both our cardiovascular health and our cognitive abilities. If you haven't had a good night's sleep in a few days, you may notice that you experience increased feelings of melancholy or irritability. If this becomes a trend for you, you may even have to cope with mental illnesses like anxiety and depression as a result of it.

The pineal gland may also have an effect on the health of our bones over time, according to some research. When the production of melatonin in our bodies slows down, we increase our risk of developing bone illnesses like osteoporosis. As a result of the fact that the pineal gland is sensitive to light, it is possible for certain people to suffer from seasonal affective disorder if they reside in areas where winters are particularly long and dark.

Both problems in the hypothalamus and an excessive calcification of the pineal gland, which is the deposit of calcium on the pineal gland, have the potential to have an effect on our pineal gland. It is possible for our circadian rhythms to be disrupted when the pineal gland is not functioning properly. Over the course of time, more symptoms may begin to appear, such as osteoporosis, which is particularly common in postmenopausal women.

Alterations that occur in relation to menstruation, ovulation, and fertility

Symptoms of nausea

Uneasy feelings

Pain in the head

Problems with one's mental health

Problems determining one's position in space

Acquiring Knowledge Of The Body's Various Energy Centers

Chakras are energy centers that are found throughout the human body and are intricately connected to one another. There are seven basic chakras, each of which is related with a particular component of our bodily, emotional, and spiritual well-being. By gaining an understanding of these energy centers, we can gain vital insights into the workings of our own internal systems, which in turn can assist us in leading lives that are more balanced and harmonious. In this piece, we will investigate the seven basic chakras, as well as the ways in which these energy centers influence our physical and mental wellness.

The first chakra, also known as the root chakra, may be found at the base of the spine. Its function is to ground and stabilize the body. Our sense of stability, security, and anchoring are all connected to this particular energy source in our bodies. When we have achieved a state of harmony in our root chakra, we are able to go through the world with more self-assurance and steadiness, as well as a sense of safety and security in our own life. Nevertheless, if there is an imbalance in the root chakra, we may suffer with feelings of anxiety, fear, and insecurity, and we may find it difficult to find our foothold in the world.

The sacral chakra, which can be found in the region of the lower belly, is the second chakra. This energy area is connected to our feeling of creativity as well as our ability to experience pleasure and sexuality. When we are able to freely and truly express ourselves, we have a sense of joy and creativity in our life, which is a sign that our sacral chakra is functioning properly and needs balancing. On the other hand, if there is an imbalance in the sacral chakra, we may have difficulties with self-expression, creativity, and intimate relationships.

The solar plexus chakra, which can be found in the upper belly, is the third of the seven chakras. Our sense of personal strength, as well as our self-esteem and self-confidence, are all connected to this energy center. We experience a sense of inner strength and self-assurance, as well as the ability to confidently stand up for ourselves in the world, when the solar plexus chakra is in a state of balance. Nevertheless, if there is an imbalance in the solar plexus chakra, we may battle with emotions of uncertainty, low self-esteem, and lack of confidence.

The area in the middle of the chest known as the heart chakra is the location of the fourth chakra. Our feelings of love, compassion, and connection are all connected to this particular energy source in our bodies. When we have harmony in our heart chakra, we are able to establish connections that are both profound and meaningful, and we experience feelings of love and connection with others around us. On the other hand, if there is an imbalance in the heart chakra, we may battle with emotions of loneliness, isolation, and disconnectedness.

The throat is the location of the fifth chakra, which is known as the throat chakra. This energy center is related with our capacity to speak clearly and to express ourselves in a way that is true to who we are. When we have achieved harmony in our throat chakra, we are able to communicate our thoughts and feelings to others in a way that is both clear and assured, as well as form meaningful bonds with those we interact with. However, when there is an imbalance in the throat chakra, we may have problems communicating properly and find it difficult to explain ourselves clearly. This can be a source of frustration.

The third eye chakra is the sixth chakra, and it is situated in the exact middle of the forehead. This energy point is connected to our innate sense of knowing, as well as our wisdom and spiritual perception. We are able to access our own inner wisdom and guidance, as well as establish a connection with our higher selves, when the third eye chakra is in a state of equilibrium. When the third eye chakra is out of alignment, on the other hand, we may battle with emotions of bewilderment, a lack of clarity, and an inability to access our intuition.

The crown chakra is the seventh and last chakra, and it may be found at the very top of the head. Our feeling of spirituality, our connection to the divine, and our higher awareness are all connected to this energy point in our bodies. When we are able to connect with our more evolved self as well as the universal consciousness, it is a sign that our crown chakra is functioning properly. Nevertheless, if there is an imbalance in the crown chakra, we may battle with emotions of alienation, a lack of purpose, and spiritual disorientation.

As a conclusion, gaining an awareness of the seven basic chakras can give us priceless insights into our own inner workings and assist us in achieving greater balance and harmony in our everyday lives. By gaining an awareness of these energy centers, we may learn to recognize when they are out of balance and then take actions to bring them back to a condition in which they are in harmony and equilibrium.

Meditation, yoga, the use of visualization, and energy healing are just few of the disciplines that can be utilized in the process of balancing and aligning the chakras; there are many other methods as well. We may begin to grow a deeper understanding of ourselves and our inner workings by implementing these practices into our day-to-day lives, and we can also develop a greater sense of serenity, balance, and harmony in our lives as a result.

In addition to these practices, it is essential to attend to our needs on a bodily, emotional, and spiritual level and to take care of ourselves in a manner that is holistic. This could include maintaining a good diet, engaging in regular physical activity, spending time in natural settings, engaging in self-care practices, and participating in pursuits that bring us joy and satisfaction.

In the end, we can reach greater levels of health, pleasure, and well-being, and live a life that is more satisfying and purposeful by knowing the energy centers of the body and taking actions to balance and align them.

The Navataras: An Explanation Of Their Meanings

The meanings and symbols that are attached to each of the Navataras offer extremely helpful insights into the characteristics and energy that are connected to them. Individuals can achieve a more profound comprehension of their own nature, the experiences of their life, and the path they are on spiritually if they take the time to learn the symbolism associated with each of the Navatara. Astrologers make use of this information to provide counsel, forecasts, and interpretations that are based on the impact exerted by each Navatara in the birth chart of a particular individual.III. A Meaning for the Navataras

A. Traits and characteristics that are related with each of the Navataras

Within the Navatara chakra system, each of the Navatarashave its own set of distinctive attributes and qualities. An in-depth analysis of each of the Navatara is presented here:

1. Janma, which is a representation of birth and a fresh start. People who are born during this period of the zodiac are typically brave, ambitious, and endowed with significant leadership abilities. They are highly successful in positions of leadership and responsibility, in addition to having the urge to launch new projects and businesses.

2. Sampat: The term "Sampat" refers to a prosperous and abundant life as well as money. People who are born during this Navatara have a natural talent for amassing and organizing their resources. They are gifted with an innate sense for business, expertise in financial concerns, and the capacity to achieve

material success in their endeavors. They frequently lead a life that is luxurious in both comfort and wealth.

3. Vipat is the personification of difficulties and impediments. Those who are born during this Navatara are doomed to encounter challenges and obstacles in a variety of facets of their lives. They are resilient, adaptable, and have the ability to make it through challenging situations successfully. They are able to emerge from these tests in a more powerful position since the obstacles contribute to their own growth and development.

4. Kshema is a name that denotes steadiness, protection, and complete happiness. Those who are born during this Navatara have a strong sense of personal safety and overall well-being throughout their life. They are naturally calm and in tune with one another, and

they create a supportive atmosphere not only for themselves but also for those in their immediate vicinity. They are typically very good at offering emotional support and sustaining healthy relationships.

5. Pratyari, also known as Pratyahara, is a symbol of metamorphosis and reflection. People who are born during this Navatara have a strong yearning for introspection and personal development on a spiritual level. They tend to engage in activities such as introspection, self-reflection, and the search for inner strength. This Navatara inspires individuals to investigate the world within, as well as to open themselves up to change on a personal level.

6. Sadhaka: Sadhaka is a term that connotes self-discipline, devotion, and personal development. People whose birth dates fall during this Navatara have

a deep-seated dedication to the process of self-improvement. They use a methodical approach and are completely committed to doing what they set out to do. They are exceptional at engaging in spiritual activities, making efforts to better themselves, and assisting others on their path.

7. Naidhana is a name that refers to challenges, tribulations, and the process of gaining wisdom. People who are born under this Navatara have a difficult time overcoming difficulties and impediments throughout their lives. Their resiliency, strength, and overall wisdom are all enhanced as a result of the lessons that they have learned as a result of these events. They acquire the skills necessary to triumph through hardship and emerge victorious.

8. Mitra is an ancient Sanskrit name that has come to mean friendliness, social

relations, and harmony. Those who are born during this Navatara have an innate capacity for developing and sustaining friendships. They are exceptional when it comes to social interactions, diplomacy, and working together. They cultivate harmonious relationships with others and work hard to achieve balance and justice in their dealings with those around them.

9. Atimitra Represents Compassion, Humanitarianism, and Selflessness Atimitra is a symbol of compassion, humanitarianism, and selflessness. People who are born in this Navatara have a tremendous desire to be of service to others as well as a profound capacity for empathy. They have a kind and kind nature, and they make significant contributions to the prosperity of the community. They exemplify the spirit of selflessness and

actively contribute to making the world a more compassionate place.

(Take a pause here for twenty seconds)

Now try to bring your consciousness back into connection with your body. Your whole physique exudes calm and ease. You do not exhibit any signs of tension in any region of your body. Your back is in a good position. Your breath is soft and soothing.

The process of clearing chakras of obstructions and healing them starts now.

Imagine that you are looking at your body through your mind's eye. Feel the sensations that are occurring throughout your body.

Sensitize yourself all the way down to the tips of your fingers. You should be able to feel a tingling sensation coming from your fingertips. Put yourself through the ice or the fire, depending on the temperature. Permit the feeling to move up to your arms, then to your shoulders, then your throat, then your head, chest, and stomach, and finally all the way down to your feet.

(There will be a ten second pause)

You are currently immersed in a sea of delicate feelings. Always keep in mind that your body is not who you are. You are unadulterated vitality. You are the undiluted state of consciousness. Your awareness takes the form of your physical body, which is the most obvious representation of it. You have to get through this crudeness in order to encounter the truth and uncover your authentic self.

There are seven energy centers located throughout your body where the energy is concentrated. To become the full expression of who you are, you must first bring each of the seven chakras into harmony.

You are about to go through the process of your consciousness moving up from the energy center with the lowest vibration to the energy center with the highest vibration. There is no requirement for you to memorize the names of the chakras or any of the information. Simply listen to the voice, and allow it to travel through your head and your body as it does so. Avoid letting your attention wander towards the realm of the chakras at any cost.

Do not allow your intellect to overthink things. Just listen, and then put the mental pictures that play through your head out of your thoughts. You should listen in a relaxed and unhurried manner.

(Take a pause for twenty seconds.) At this point, bring your awareness to the center of who you are, at the base of your spine. This is symbolized by the

Muladhara chakra, also known as the root chakra. Muladhara is the level at which your consciousness is most obviously manifest. If you want to know what it's like to be free from the constraints of the material world, you have to learn to transcend it.

It is a symbol of your lack of knowledge. Because of your ignorance, you behave in a slothful manner. When this energy area is not active, you may experience feelings of lethargy. If there is a blockage in the Muladhara chakra, you will feel lethargic. Permit your thoughts to wander through the recent history you've experienced.

How were you feeling about an hour ago? Try not to stiffen up either your body or your mind. Allow the events of the preceding hour to run through your mind.

(Take a pause here for twenty seconds)

Reenact the occurrences that were place so that you can see what happened. Just sit back and observe without making any kind of move. These thoughts that you are having right now are emanating from within your own mind, and not from any other source in the outside world. These thoughts are an outward expression of who you are on the inside.

Maintain vigilance. In the same manner as if you were watching a movie. Think back to the events that took place two hours ago, three hours ago, the day before, one week ago, and one month ago.

Recognizing And Appreciating One's Physical Form Through Self-Love, Self-Care, And Body Positivity

Our physical bodies are vehicles for the sensual and spiritual expression that we are. When we embrace our sensuality and work to cultivate a profound connection with our senses, one of the most important things we can do is to respect and take care of our bodies. When we show our bodies love and care, we cultivate an environment that is conducive to sensual inquiry and the process of coming into one's own. You can show respect for your body and commit to practicing self-care by doing the following:

Engage in Regular Practices of Self-Care:

Set aside a specific amount of time each day to engage in activities that are beneficial to your overall health and well-being, such as taking a soothing bath, engaging in some light yoga practice, or treating yourself to a pampering skincare routine.

Establish a bedtime routine that promotes deep rejuvenation and restoration, and make getting plenty of restful sleep a top priority.

Participate in actions that are beneficial to your physical health, such as going for regular exercise, eating nutritious meals, and keeping yourself well-hydrated.

Cultivate a Positive Attitude Towards Your Body Make a mental shift toward accepting your body as it is and revel in the extraordinary beauty and capabilities that it possesses.

Surround yourself with people and things that are positive about your body, such as following people and accounts on social media that encourage self-love and diverse body representations.

Practices involving the use of a mirror and positive affirmations can help you learn to accept and appreciate your body just the way it is right now.

Embrace Your Sensual Self-Expression: Experiment with a variety of different forms of self-expression that honor your body and sensuality, such as dance, creative arts, or sensual movement practices such as belly dancing or pole dancing.

Dress in a way that brings you closer in touch with your sensual side while also boosting your self-assurance and comfort levels.

Engage in practices of self-touch and self-pleasure, with the goal of cultivating a deeper understanding of, and connection with, the desires and responses of your body.

You can create a nurturing environment for your body to thrive in by practicing self-care, being positive about your body, and loving yourself. This will allow your senses to be reawakened, and your sensual self will be able to flourish.

The Strength Of One's Own Suggestions

This Speak Chakra can be of assistance in the process of giving form to a thought when it comes time to do so. The only way for thoughts to materialize is through the Speak Chakra. This Chakra contains an incredible amount of power. Through the use of self-suggestions, we are able to create our own form through the use of this Chakra.

Whatever we say about ourselves is what we ultimately become. When we begin to speak, even if that is not who we are, we transform into that. This rule applies to each and every person, as well as to one's own body, to the bodies of other people, and even to trees and animals. Because man does not know this secret, he uses the power of Speak Chakra without even realizing it, leading to his own demise.

When an army chief issues an order to his troops, the entirety of the army immediately executes that order. In precisely the same way, the impact of using Speak Chakra is directly felt throughout our existence. For instance, you have to have done this at some point: on a day off, when you wake up early in the morning, you have to have told yourself something along the lines of, "Today is a day of rest; there is no work; there is no hurry; I will do everything at my leisure." A holiday is being observed today.

Therefore, on that day, you must have noticed its effect in your normal routine, which is completely beyond your ability to control.

Because you want to relax and take it easy first, you put off doing the majority of the work until later. You won't be able to rely on your body to support you, and you might get the urge to relax even further. despite the fact that you had a restful sleep the night before. You exhibited an utter lack of tension. You have unknowingly given yourself the incorrect suggestions, and as a result, you are now feeling as though you need to get more rest.

Perhaps at some point in the past you have reflected to yourself, "today I am tired, today I am not feeling well, and today I am not in the mood." When you say this to yourself unconsciously in your mind, you must have noticed that your entire body will feel tired on that particular day.

The explanation for this is that the Speak Chakra communicates its orders to the thyroid gland, which then relays them to all of the body's millions of trillions of cells, which are collectively performing the duties of an army.

And on the very day that you are experiencing these feelings, the executive director of your company gives you a call first thing in the morning. You are obligated to go because he requests that you come to the office immediately to assist with some extremely time-sensitive work that can only be completed by you.

After making the decision to go, you begin rationalizing your departure by telling yourself things like "I have to work, I need to arrive on time, there is nothing wrong with me, I am healthy," and so on. As soon as you begin issuing such commands to yourself, you will begin to experience a return of your previous sense of power. And you get ready in such a hurry that you beat the morning deadline and arrive at the office early. You will complete that work and then you will also return home. But even after coming home you will not feel tired. This is the direct effect of the Speak Chakra.

What caused it to occur?

When you exert positive willpower and give yourself positive commands, your glands, your brain, and all of the cells in your body immediately begin to obey you. You begin to sense the strength that lies within yourself. Your entire cellular army obeys and complies with your instruction.

Let us take a look at one more occurrence that falls under this category.

Imagine that one day you are out walking on the road, and in addition to being exhausted, you are also ill, and you lack the strength to continue going. In such a scenario, you notice a dog barking its way quickly approaching you from someplace in the distance. What steps do you take when this occurs? You undoubtedly got your feet moving as soon as you caught sight of the dog in order to get away from it, right? Even if you are too weak to walk or if you are sick, if you see that dog you will be able to get away from there quickly. Where did you get all that power from that you were able to start jogging so quickly? Because at that moment you became aware that at this time it is very vital to run in order to save yourself, and because you ran at that time, you saved yourself. There is a significant risk, so get away as quickly as you can. If you don't run, the dog will hurt you. There is no other option. As soon as we issue this command to ourselves, our brain and every cell in our body immediately begin obeying that command in accordance with the terms of that command.

So the question is, where did all of this strength originate from? How was it that the person who felt so weak that they couldn't even walk started running? Who or what was the source of that power? Your own thoughts and ideas are the exclusive and exclusive source of that power. What we tell ourselves over and over again shapes who we are.

Another thing that we need to find out about is the origin of the words. Where did they come from? Which came first, the words or the thought?

The mouth is the organ through which we communicate, but the mind is where it all begins.

Auto-suggestions are mental messages that are constantly being repeated to oneself, either consciously or unconsciously, by every human being. They will only benefit from these auto-suggestions if they choose to view them in a good light. Or, if it is unfavourable, it can turn out to be a curse.

The Law Of Cause And Effect Is Associated With The Root Chakra- Karma

Due to the fact that this chakra governs your ability to live and provide for your fundamental requirements, when it is out of alignment, you are likely to experience feelings of being ungrounded, insecure, worried, and nervous.

Karma refers to any act, activity, or deed in which the goals and outputs of an individual (the cause) have an effect on the future of that individual (the effect). In essence, having a good intention and carrying out good deeds contributes to having excellent and happier outcomes. On the other hand, having terrible intentions and carrying out bad actions both contribute to having bad results. The concept of coming back to one's previous life, also known as rebirth, suggests that the choices you make in the here and now will determine your future. People also frequently say that there are repercussions for their acts. According to the theory known as the Law of Cause and Effect, every action has a corresponding result from a purely physical point of view. Therefore, the decisions you make and the actions you take may have consequences that you could never have imagined. The same is true for the energy that resides within you. Nothing except good can result from having a constructive outlook on life and channelling negative energy towards constructive ends. On the other hand, the opposite is also true.

Consequently, when it comes time to make a decision, it is essential to think about each alternative and how the energy of your body reacts to it. Is it anything that excites you? Do you sense excitement and vitality as a result of the option? If this is the case, then energy is flowing easily. It is likely that performing such an action will result in a positive and helpful outcome, not just for you but also for a large number of other people. The converse is also true: if a choice causes you anxiety and worry, the outcomes might not be as satisfying for you or for others.

It is possible to turn a bad sensation into something positive if you put your mind to it. You might, for instance, be feeling angry yet be able to transform that energy by doing something like going for a run or a walk outside in the fresh air. This not only makes your body healthier, but it also eliminates any negative energy that may be present and rebalances the energy that is already there in the body.

Your body analyses every activity in terms of the chance that it will fulfil your requirements for safety and security, or in terms of the heightened amount of hazard it poses. Your connection to the earth, which is maintained by the root chakra, as well as essential information about how grounded or threatened you feel in relation to the acts you choose, are both communicated to you. When you have faith that the earth will take care of you, you might experience a sense of safety and well-being that guides you towards the most effective courses of action to follow. It is a positive sign that the energy in your chakras is balanced when you find yourself pondering your actions and making sure they are for the greatest good.

Developing A Sacred Environment

Establishing a sacred location is one of the most important steps in getting ready for a chakra healing session. Your chakra healing practises, your ability to connect with your inner self, and your capacity to undergo profound transformation can all be enhanced by the presence of a dedicated room that functions as a holy space. In this chapter, we will discuss the components and procedures necessary to create a holy place that is conducive to your chakra healing journey and will provide support for it. You can create an atmosphere that strengthens your connection to the divine and promotes significant healing and development in yourself and others via careful planning, construction, and care of this holy space.

The Process of Choosing the Space:

Choose an area in your house to serve as the location of your personal sacred space. It could be a separate room, a secluded nook, or any other space in the house that provides the opportunity for alone and peace. When selecting the location, keep the following considerations in mind:

Privacy: During your chakra healing practise, select a location in which you will not be disturbed as much and where you will have the opportunity to maintain your privacy.

Comfort: Ensure that the setting is comfortable and welcoming, with sufficient sitting or cushions for meditation or relaxation.

Selecting a Location That Receives Natural Light It is best, if at all feasible, to pick a location that gets natural light as this can help to improve the vibe and atmosphere of the sacred space. You also have the option of employing softer lighting to bring about the desired calming effect.

Before you begin to create your sacred place, it is necessary to remove and cleanse the energy of the surrounding environment. This should be done in the same room or nearby. This procedure expels any negative or stale energy, so transforming the surrounding space into one that is pure and holy. The following are some strategies that can be used to clear and clean the space:

Smudging: To cleanse the area, burn some white sage, palosanto, or any other sacred herb, and then move the smoke about in a clockwise pattern.

The use of bells, chimes, singing bowls, or any other type of musical instrument to make resonant sounds and fill the area with positive vibrations is an effective method of sound cleansing.

Visualisation: Picture a brilliant, pristine white light sweeping through the area, illuminating and sanitising every nook and cranny.

Having an Objective in Mind:

Establish a crystal-clear purpose for the sacred area you have created. You can make this intention very particular to your chakra healing path, or you can make it more general for overall healing and spiritual development. You might find it helpful to write down your aim and keep a copy of it in your holy space so that you are constantly reminded of its significance.

Choosing Decorations With Meaning:

Choose pieces of decor for your space that have a spiritual significance and a resonance with your chakra healing journey. Some suggestions for significant decorations are as follows:

The Properties of Crystals and Gemstones: Put crystals and gemstones that correspond to each of your chakras in the sacred place you have created. For instance, amethyst is associated with the crown chakra, rose quartz is associated with the heart chakra, and citrine is associated with the solar plexus chakra.

Symbolic Representations: Be sure to incorporate any symbolic representations that are significant to you, such as pictures of gods and goddesses, mandalas, yantras, or sacred geometry.

Plants & Flowers: Bringing the vibrancy and energy of nature into your sacred area can be accomplished by including either living plants or freshly cut flowers.

Displaying inspiring quotations, affirmations, or mantras that resonate with your healing path can provide you with daily reminders of your objectives and aspirations. These can be in the form of quotes, affirmations, or mantras.

Awareness Of The Heart Chakra Through The Use Of Crystals And Essential Oils

We are related to both the Earth and the universal life force energy that is all around us, as was covered in the books that came before this one. Our energy is connected to the energy of natural creations such as crystals and essential oils because these things are also products of the earth's natural processes. Both pure crystals and essential oils emit vibrations at specific frequencies; these frequencies can be used to tune specific centres in your energy system.

Through their vibrations, colour frequency, and fragrances, the stones and oils that will be explained below have the ability to clear energetic blockages and bring balance to the Heart chakra when utilised on a regular basis and with the intention to do so.

CRYSTALS That Help Awaken the Heart Chakra by Way of Their Colour Frequencies and Vibrations

The crystal known as the "stone of unconditional love" is rose quartz, which also happens to be my personal favourite. Rose quartz is the crystal that rules the heart chakra and all other pink crystals. It is a pink gemstone that radiates compassion and is gentle, soft, and kind in appearance. It is the ideal stone for cultivating compassion in all its forms, including self-compassion, compassion for others, empathy, and forgiveness.

Rhodonite is a stunning gemstone that is typically found in varying colours of light pink and red, with occasional areas of black. As a result of this, this stone is a very potent Heart and Root chakra balancer. Rhodonite fosters the development of a solid base, which makes it much simpler to clear space in the heart, as well as to maintain a position of trust and compassion. This precious stone is frequently described to a pair of rose-colored glasses because it enables one to view the world through the prism of love, compassion, and understanding.

Green Jade: Green Jade is a type of jade that is commonly referred to as a "luck stone" because it is believed to have the ability to assist in the opening of one's heart space, allowing one to more effectively manifest their ideal life. Because the frequencies of this stone are so closely matched with the vibratory level of the Heart chakra, it is able to assist in the shifting of obstructions and the clearing of those blockages in order to facilitate a healthy flow of energy through this centre.

Green Tourmaline: The vibrations of green tourmaline are said to assist raise compassion, free the Heart area of judgement and other blockages, and strengthen the physical power of your heart. Green tourmaline is also known as the "compassion stone." This precious stone is a potent instrument that can assist in re-establishing a connection between your heart core and the world below your feet, all around you, and above you.

Emerald: Emerald is a gorgeous shade of royal green, and its vibrations inspire energies of harmony and balanced love (with yourself and others). Emerald is a precious gemstone. It is known as a "prophecy stone" and has the ability to assist you in connecting with your own inner wisdom and learning to trust the messages that come from your Heart centre.

Green Aventurine: This deep green gemstone is a compassionate healer that helps us reach into higher levels of inner peace and harmony with others. Green Aventurine is associated with the heart chakra. This stone facilitates a more profound connection with the natural world, the people in our immediate environment, and our own inner world. Green Aventurine is also thought to assist in opening the heart centre, making it simpler to draw love to oneself as well as to give and accept it.

Malachite: Malachite is a beautiful green and black stone that is known to help with the two key criteria for openly and effortlessly giving and receiving love: having a clear heart and a clear voice. This is the reason why this stone is connected to both the Heart chakra and the Throat chakra. Malachite: Malachite is a beautiful stone that helps with the two important factors for openly and effortlessly giving and receiving love.

Chrysoprase is a stone that is a vivid shade of green and is renowned for its ability to revitalise one's heart centre. Chrysoprase facilitates our transition from codependence into a position where we may forgive ourselves, have compassion for ourselves, and love ourselves more deeply. This precious stone is also known as the "stone of divine truth," and it is said to facilitate a connection with our higher selves, our souls, and the truth.

As we've covered in earlier volumes, one of the most effective methods to permit the crystal vibrations to link with your own energy is to wear crystal jewellery on the skin. This is one of the greatest ways to do this. The benefits of the stones can be continuously absorbed in this entertaining manner. During meditation, you may also lay one of these gemstones on your heart centre by lying down and positioning it in the middle of your chest. This will allow the stone to open your heart and cleanse your energy. Be sure to get your intention straight before beginning the meditation on the Heart chakra; you can do this by reciting one of the affirmations from the chapter before this one. Maintain your attention on this affirmation and the space in your heart. You might also try saying any heart-opening affirmations while holding a gemstone that corresponds to your Heart chakra in your hand.

Just having these Heart healing crystals in your presence during challenging times may be enough for them to help clear your Heart space and bring loving and compassionate energies to the surface. This is especially true if you are aware that you are struggling with issues that stem from an imbalance in the Heart centre (such as feeling lonely or isolated, being envious, or being codependent, for example). When writing in your gratitude notebook or engaging in a reflective exercise based on the Heart chakra questions and prompts found in chapter 3, it is a wonderful idea to keep a Heart chakra crystal either on your person or in close proximity to you.

You can also position gemstones and crystals associated with your Heart chakra throughout your house to assist in the creation of a balanced energy flow through both your physical space and your Heart centre. If you want to foster compassion and harmony in your house, one way to do so is to decorate with crystals that correspond to the heart chakra and place them in common areas and bedrooms. You might also try having a soothing bath with the crystals associated with your Heart chakra in order to bring gentle healing energies of love, trust, and forgiveness.

Keep in mind that the crystals or gemstone jewellery you wear might become "clogged up" with energy, especially if you use them on a regular basis. Crystals can be purified by submerging them in water, rubbing them with sage or another powerful herb, or even utilising other "cleansing" crystals like selenite. These methods can be used to clear any energy that has been stagnant. It is important to keep in mind that activating the selenite with the goal of cleansing your crystals should come first. You may also reset and cleanse a crystal by cupping it in your hands and then blowing three gusts of air into your palms. This can be done with a piece of jewellery as well.

If you use your crystals frequently, you may find that you need to charge them more frequently than once every several months. Before you use them again, you should make sure that they have been charged if they have been idle for an extended period of time. Crystals and jewellery made of gemstones need to be charged so that they may function at their maximum potential and help facilitate the flow of energy via the heart. For ease of tracking, you can cleanse and charge your crystals at the same time; but, for optimal results, you should aim to cleanse and charge your crystals at least once every two months. In addition, one can utilise selenite to charge other types of crystals. In addition to this, I expose my crystals to either the sun or the moon in order to allow them to charge. You can also use the vibrations produced by a singing bowl, drums, bells, or any other kind of sound therapy to clear, reset, and charge the energy contained within your crystals if you have access to any of these instruments.

The First Chakras, Also Known As The Root Chakras

The energy trip through the subtle body starts with the first chakra, which is the foundation chakra. Its name in Sanskrit translates to "root." It belongs to the Earth category. It is necessary for life. It is an honourable thing "To Have." This location serves as a repository for the Kundalini energy. This is the location of physical health, groundedness, stability, youthful quality, vigour, the instinct to either fight or flee for one's life, and financial success.

It is said that the colour red is related with this chakra. It is situated near the bottom of the spine and stores the energy that is found there in addition to that which surrounds the gonads, feet, and legs. It is associated with your ability to smell, which is the very first sense that you are conscious of when you are born.

When your root chakra is in harmony, you will feel safe, prosperous, at ease with who you are, centred, peaceful, and grounded, and you will have a strong connection to the natural world and the earth.

When there is an imbalance in your root chakra, you may have feelings of insecurity, anger, alienation, despair, lack of patience, anxiousness, greed, unneeded fear, and a lack of abundance. When this imbalance becomes apparent in our bodies, it might take the form of recurrent illnesses, obesity, eating disorders, constipation, knee problems, sciatica, or even haemorrhoids.

It is essential to have an understanding of the root chakra, as this is the location of the dormant Kundalini energy, which, once awakened, will ascend from this chakra. It is also essential to understand the root chakra's link to the other chakras. But one must be careful not to place too much emphasis on this energy, and here is why: The Kundalini awakening starts here, although it may also finish at the root chakra if it continues down to that level. Some people's experiences suggest that it is the chakra that takes the longest to fully awaken. It is possible that the rest of the change through the chakras will take place first; nevertheless, in order to attain genuine balance, the energy of Kundalini must return to the beginning, to the place where the source of the energy awakening initially appeared.

7. Awakening Prosperity: An Introduction to Prosperity Healing [7. Awakening Prosperity]

Pranic Healing has a number of sub-specialties, one of which is known as Prosperity Healing. This sub-specialty of Pranic Healing focuses on bringing one's life more success, financial wealth, and general prosperity. It is predicated on the realisation that our mental states, feelings, and energetic patterns have a substantial influence on the extent to which we are able to amass riches and enjoy monetary security in our lives.

In order to remove spiritual blocks and imbalances that may be preventing abundance from flowing freely, it is necessary for us to energise the body's chakras as part of the Prosperity Healing process. If we purify and energise the various energy centres, also known as chakras, we can improve the flow of energy throughout the body, so increasing our capacity to take in and make use of the energy associated with wealth.

The employment of particular Pranic Healing protocols is required for prosperity healing techniques. These protocols include scanning, purifying, energising, and balancing the energy centres that are connected with prosperity. These energy centres include the Basic Chakra (also known as the Root Chakra), the Solar Plexus Chakra, and the Crown Chakra. These strategies serve to remove stagnant or negative energy patterns connected to scarcity, lack, and limiting beliefs, and replace them with positive, abundant, and prosperous energies. This is accomplished by replacing the energies with which they are replaced with positive, abundant, and prosperous energies.

During a session of success Healing, I also offer assistance on the kinds of practical acts, financial planning, and mental adjustments that are helpful in bringing about material manifestations of success. This can include tips on goal setting, affirmations, visualisation techniques, and other methods, as well as actionable activities to effectively attract and make use of financial resources.

It is essential to keep in mind that Prosperity Healing is neither a quick fix or a magical answer to issues pertaining to one's finances. It is a holistic strategy that combines energetic work with practical actions, allowing individuals to connect their energy, ideas, and actions to create a fertile ground for prosperity to bloom. Because it is a holistic approach, it mixes energetic work with practical actions. To acquire benefits that are sustainable over time, it is generally recommended to practise on a constant and regular basis.

Acquiring Expertise in the Correct Pronunciation Acquiring expertise in the correct pronunciation of mantras requires patience, practise, and direction. The following is a list of important steps and strategies that will assist you in achieving perfect pronunciation:

1. Learn from an experienced teacher: If at all possible, it is best to learn mantras and the correct way to pronounce them from an instructor who is qualified and has prior knowledge of the specific tradition and language. Individualised instruction and correction of any articulation issues you may have can be provided by a teacher.

2. Break Down the Mantra The next step is to take the mantra and carefully break it down into its individual syllables and sounds. It would be helpful if you could get familiar with the pronunciation of

each syllable and understand how its acceptable enunciation should sound.

3. Listen and Repeat: Chant along with experienced practitioners or listen to audio recordings of them chanting. Hearing correct pronunciation enables you to better absorb the sounds and reproduce them correctly in your own speech.

4. Make Use of Phonetic Transliterations: If the mantra is written in a script that you are not familiar with, such as Sanskrit, then you should make use of phonetic transliterations to assist you in correctly reciting the syllables. These transliterations represent the sounds of the mantra using the alphabets most commonly used.

5. Conduct your practise with care and gentleness: To begin, begin by repeating the mantra in a care and kind manner.

It is important that you pay attention to the how each syllable sounds as well as how it feels when you say it.

As you become more at ease with the pronunciation, gradually pick up the rate that you're speaking at.

6. Make a recording of yourself: Make a recording of yourself chanting and pay close attention to it. Check it against the way it's pronounced in audio recordings or by people who are considered to be experts in the field. You may realise through this self-evaluation that there are areas in which you may improve.

7. Ask for input: Make sure you ask your instructor or other experienced practitioners for input. Your pronunciation will improve along with your chanting ability thanks to their guidance as well as their critical feedback.

8. Become familiar with the rules of pronunciation: Before beginning to chant, it is important to study some instances of how the holy language you are using is spoken. The pronunciation and stress of syllables in a given language are determined by a set of phonetic principles that are exclusive to that language.

9. Make practise a regular part of your schedule A methodical approach is essential for picking up proper pronunciation. Make sure you give yourself enough time every day to chant mantras so that you can hone your skills and absorb the positive vibes.

10. Develop a sense of dedication by approaching the recitation of mantras with a sense of commitment and reverence. Your purpose might be furthered and your energy can become

one with the holy music if you have a genuine connection with the chant.

Healing Through Chakras And How It Affects Relationships

Additionally, the chakras have the potential to play a significant part in the relationships in our lives. The energy that flows through our chakras has an effect on how we connect with other people, how we interact, and how we express ourselves. Having an awareness of the chakras can facilitate the development of more fulfilling relationships and a more profound sense of connection with the people we care about.

The chakras not only have an effect on the interactions we have with other people, but they also have a strong connection to our thoughts, attitudes, and perceptions of the world that is going on around us. Blockages or imbalances in these energy centres can manifest as negative thought patterns, limiting beliefs, and difficult emotions. Each chakra is associated with a distinct mental and emotional state, and blockages or imbalances in these energy centres can cause blockages or imbalances. Bringing our chakras into harmony and aligning them can help us create a more optimistic and open-minded approach, which in turn can assist us in developing more meaningful connections with the people and circumstances that are a part of our lives.

The significance of maintaining a healthy Chakra balance in intimate relationships

Maintaining a good balance in your chakras is essential for having successful relationships. When we have achieved harmony in each of our chakras, we are better able to communicate openly and truthfully with those we hold dearest, as well as with ourselves. On the other hand, if our chakras are blocked or out of balance, we may have trouble communicating, expressing ourselves, or connecting with our partners. This might make it difficult for us to communicate.

The Application of Chakra Healing to Solve Relationship Problems

Healing of the chakras can be an effective method for resolving problems in interpersonal relationships. We are able to clear energy blockages and match our energy with that of our partner if we put in the effort to bring each chakra into balance and to awaken it. When dealing with relationship problems, one method to employ chakra healing is to concentrate on the chakras that are related with that particular issue. For instance, if we have difficulty communicating with our significant other, we might direct our attention towards balancing and opening our throat chakra.

Healing Relationships Through the Integration of Chakra Practises

Including chakra healing as part of our relationship practise can assist us in developing deeper connections with the people we care about and bettering the quality of our connections overall. Partner chakra meditations are one technique that can be utilised to bring chakra healing into our connection with one another. During this meditation, both partners concentrate on balancing and awakening each other's chakras, which can contribute to the development of a more profound sense of connection and harmony.

How can working with my chakras help me improve my health, my relationships, and achieve the goals I have set for myself?

Working with your chakras is an effective method for attaining your goals, as well as improving your health and relationships. By gaining an understanding of your chakra system and actively engaging with it, you may correct imbalances in your energy field and improve your general health. Performing chakra work can assist enhance your life in a number of ways, including the following:

Work with the chakras can assist in the improvement of one's physical health by correcting imbalances that may contribute to the development of illness or disease. By way of illustration, working with the heart chakra can assist in the improvement of cardiovascular health as well as the reduction of tension and worry. Developing one's relationship with the root chakra can assist in the general promotion of physical anchoring and stability.

Relationships: Working with your chakras can also assist enhance your relationships by addressing imbalances that may be affecting your capacity to connect with other people. This can help you feel more connected to the people in your life. For instance, working on one's throat chakra can assist increase one's ability to communicate and express themselves, whilst working on one's heart chakra can help foster compassion and empathy.

Chakra work can assist you in accomplishing your goals by fostering balance and alignment within your energy system and between your goals and your energy system. For instance, working with the solar plexus chakra can help develop confidence and self-esteem, and working with the third eye chakra can help improve visualisation and manifestation. Both of these benefits can be achieved by working with the chakras. Consider incorporating activities such as meditation, yoga, energy healing, or visualisation exercises into your life in order to work on balancing your chakras. You may also choose to collaborate with a practitioner who specialises in chakra work in order to establish a personalised practise that caters to your specific requirements and objectives.

The Chakra Of Verbal Expression

Because there are so many ways that humans can interact with one another, it is fair to say that communication is one of the more difficult aspects of being human. We express ourselves and our opinions through artistic means such as painting, drawing, and sculpting. We verbally communicate our feelings to our spouse when he or she does something that upsets us; we behaviorally communicate our thoughts to others when we roll our eyes or shrug our shoulders; we communicate information through written symbols and language; and we communicate knowledge through written symbols and language.

The Throat Chakra is the wellspring of the energy that underlies the complexity of communication. You may have already surmised this, but the energy node associated with the Throat may be found—you guessed it—in our throats. Because it is located within our throat's vocal chords, the majority of the Throat exercises that you will come across will focus on activities that cause our vocal chords to vibrate, such as speaking, humming, singing, gurgling, yelling, and other similar sounds. In addition to its location in our bodies, the Throat is responsible for an extremely significant aspect of our lives: communication. This Chakra governs how much we are able to express ourselves, how freely our creativity flows, how strong our personal will is, how much we know about ourselves, how intuitive we are, how well we can listen, and how well we can take criticism.

The Throat is the energy source that enables us to communicate our thoughts, feelings, opinions, and ideas to the outside world. It also allows us to express our emotions. One may say that it is one of the energy sources within our body that maintains our sanity and that it is responsible for keeping us from going insane. After all, if we were unable to interact with one another and were compelled to keep all of our feelings, thoughts, and ideas to ourselves, we would eventually lose our minds.

The Unity of the Mind and Body

Have you ever observed that in addition to being more likely to be irritable when you are hungry, you are also more likely to be irritated?

Have you noticed that you are much more prone to become physically ill when you are under a lot of stress, when you are unhappy, or when you are depressed?

In the same way that Western science is just beginning to grasp the idea that the mind and the body are inseparable from one another, Eastern science has always been aware of the fact that the mind and the body make up a single entity. What you think and feel has an effect on the body, and vice versa: how you behave, what you eat, and what you do to fill your time all have an effect on your feelings, your thought patterns, and ultimately, your confidence and your level of productivity.

The ancients believed that the mind and the body were entwined due to a subtle body that connected the two, and they believed that this connection was caused by the subtle body. In different cultures, this vital energy was referred to as chi, qi, or prana, and it was believed to be the force that kept the universe alive. In the modern world, we are able to understand it just as readily as subatomic vibration or the transfer of pure energy. As far as we are aware, all atoms and particles, whether they appear to be material or not, are composed of energy.

It is possible to think of the chakras as the energetic 'organs' of this subtle body. They function as connectors between the mind and the body. If you are having problems or ailments with your body, then there is a fairly significant chance that there is an energetic imbalance somewhere in your body. It's possible that you're struggling with negative feelings and poor self-worth, or that you have profound, unresolved issues that you need to find a balance for.

When we deal directly with the chakras, we may address these feelings and beliefs and bring this subtle and physical body into a healthy whole. This is accomplished by bringing the chakras into alignment with one another.

THE PART THAT PRIMARY CHAKRAS AND SECONDARY CHAKRAS PLAY IN THE SYSTEM

These energy centres, known as chakras, are said to resemble spinning wheels and are dispersed throughout the body at various points. We also talk about chakras in the shape of flowers, each of which has a different number of petals. Because of this, we talk about "opening" and "closing" a chakra in the same way that we talk about opening and closing the petals of a flower.

There are seven primary chakras as well as numerous secondary and minor chakras. The chakras in the shoulders, elbows, wrists, and fingers are connected to the heart chakra, while the chakras in the hips, knees, ankles, toes, and feet are connected at the first chakra, also known as the root chakra or chakra of the base.

In order for the body to be stable, there needs to be a proper balance between the lower chakras and the upper chakras, as well as between the chakras that are positioned directly under the chakra of the heart and those that are located above.

Whether or not the energy flows properly in a person and whether or not a chakra is working in harmony with an endocrine gland, both of these factors influence the emotional and relational roles that each chakra performs.

The endocrine glands secrete hormones into the bloodstream, which in turn have an effect on the individual's emotional and mental state.

When all of the chakras are working as they should, a person will have a sense of well-being as well as the sensation of knowing their place in the universe. On the other hand, a psychological imbalance will lead to a decline in the chakras.

If one of the chakras does not have enough energy, it will draw it in from another chakra, which will cause an imbalance because the functioning of some chakras acts on that of other chakras. This is why it is essential to keep the chakras in balance because they function as communicating vessels. The energy circulates between them through communication channels known as nadis.

Utilisation of solid colours for the fabrics

This is a straightforward method for increasing your radiant energy and restoring balance to your key chakras. Because it is so simple and you can carry it out all by yourself, this is something that can be done on a daily basis. You only need to acquire some square pieces of clothing in a variety of chakra colours, and then you should proceed as follows:

1. Locate a calm, distraction-free location where you may concentrate on this activity for a maximum of ten to fifteen minutes.

2. Place a mat on the floor and lie down on your back on it. Bring out the seven items of clothing in your closet that have hues that correspond to the seven primary chakras. That consists of the colours (red, violet, orange, green, indigo, yellow, and blue).

3. With your eyes closed, bring your attention to the present now, relax your body and mind, and take numerous

slow, deep breaths for around five minutes.

4. While you are in a state of relaxation, think back on everything that has happened throughout the day, beginning with the most recent occurrence and working your way all the way back to the beginning of the day. Make sure that you go over every aspect of the previous day in detail.

5. Recognise and name all of the different feelings and attitudes that you experienced throughout the day. Locate the chakras that may have been harmed as a result of the aforementioned thoughts and feelings.

6. Once you have completed the appropriate evaluation, take the piece of cloth that corresponds to the wounded chakra and place it on the area of the body that contains that chakra.

7. While you are still lying on your back and the coloured swatch is still placed on top of the chakra point, close your eyes and attempt to imagine that the colour from the cloth is being sucked into your body and absorbed by that particular chakra. You need to bring your attention back into focus and process the fact that the balancing of your chakras is currently occurring, as well as the fact that all of the body organs and systems associated with that chakra are also getting balanced. You should do this as soon as possible.

8. While you concentrate on bringing the colour from the fabric swatch into your chakra, be sure to take a few long, deep breaths to assist you in bringing your chakras back into balance.

Repeat the practise for each of the chakras until you feel as though you have achieved equilibrium.

After you have ensured that this is the case and that your chakras are in a state of equilibrium, you will need to harmonise and strengthen them by performing the activities listed below.

1. Place each article of clothing of a different colour on top of the chakra point that corresponds to that colour on the body.

2. Take a few deep breaths and allow your body to soak up the rainbow energies that are emanating from your colourful clothing.

3. As you continue to relax on your back and take in the colours, direct your whole attention to the fact that the energy in your chakras is being re-established, reinforced, and harmonised. Feel yourself coming back into complete harmony with the world around you, and be certain that each and every part of your body is being healed, re-adjusted, and fortified as your chakra centres continue to take in the colours.

4. You also have the option of keeping those articles of clothing on your body for ten to fifteen minutes, or until you

experience a state in which you are fully aligned, charged, and balanced.

The following are some further successful applications of colour therapy for achieving chakra balancing:

*Wearing coloured garments that relate to a certain chakra colour: If you have a chakra that has been hurt, you can heal it by wearing clothes with the colour associated with the chakra that has been injured. Wearing clothing in the colour green is one way to help mend an imbalance in your heart chakra, for instance.

*Incorporating coloured lighting into your space You can utilise stained glass or light bulbs of various colours within your space in order to assist in the balancing of your chakras.

Use of natural colours: Another option open to you is to decorate your house or any other area you frequent on a regular basis with colours taken directly from nature. You are free to utilise plants and flowers of a variety of colours at any point. Even if there is an imbalance in your solar plexus chakra, you should not be afraid to let natural light directly from the sun enter your space.

Use of candles of light colours: Choose the colour you want for a candle of the relevant chakra you want to balance, and then as the candle burns, you can perform any other exercise that balances chakras, such as yoga.

Cat And Cow Pose, Also Known As Marjaryasana-Bitilasana

Begin by getting down on your hands and knees, positioning your arms so that they are squarely under your shoulders and your knees so that they are in line with your hips. Take a look at the void that exists between your palms.

Inhale deeply and slowly.

Lift your back and slowly arch your spine as you exhale. Do this as slowly as you can. Bring your chin closer to your chest while you do so. Maintain a relaxed state in your butt.

Maintain the position for a few of seconds.

After that, flow into the cow position farther down the page.

Take a deep breath in, then exhale as you slowly lift your chin and tilt your head backward. Raise your buttocks while bending forward at the waist to form an arch.

After performing each pose anywhere from five to six times, slowly bring your body back to the neutral tabletop position.

The Supine Bound Angle Pose, also referred to as SuptaBaddhaKonasana

To begin, roll over onto your back and softly lay down on the floor.

You should go into a kneeling position and bring your feet together.

Move your knees outward away from your hips and towards the floor in a controlled manner until you reach a position that is comfortable for you. If you let go of all of your tension and completely relax, you might be able to bring both of your knees down to the floor.

In that case, you always have the option of placing blocks beneath your knees for additional support.

Maintain a 45-degree angle with your arms in relation to the floor, palms pointing upward.

A bolster is another option for providing support for both your back and your head. When people first start out, a lot of them use these kinds of props since it helps them avoid damage.

While you focus on relaxing and keeping your eyes closed, you will get the most out of this pose. Take some time to relax in this position. You can do this pose either before or after your yoga practise, depending on your preference.

The "Vishuddha" Within the throat is located the Throat Chakra.

"A circle contained within a descending triangle" is the symbol.

The Vishuddha chakra is the one that deals with purification. It is connected to the ability to hear and is situated on a nerve that can be discovered in the area of the throat that is close to the pharynx. This chakra is concerned with one's capacity for learning, taking responsibility for one's own actions, having faith in oneself and one's intuition, and being creative. In the event that this particular Chakra is not healed, a wide variety of distinct physical issues may manifest in the body. This can manifest itself in a variety of ways, such as swollen glands and gums, issues with hearing, clenching and grinding of the teeth, ulcers in the mouth, and swollen glands. When this chakra is in harmony, as it should be, a person is able to have pleasant feelings and expressions, as well as good decision-making skills, creativity, and contentment in their lives. Essential oils derived from eucalyptus and sage are the ones that are thought to be most beneficial to this particular chakra.

A deficiency in the throat chakra can result in anxiety, stress, and stiffness in the neck. If you want to strengthen this chakra, you need to make sure that your food is well balanced, that you meditate on a daily basis, and that you, of course, practise yoga. Those who want to stimulate the activity of this chakra should also keep their bodies hydrated by drinking plenty of water. Shoulder openers, neck stretches, and yoga positions like the Bridge Pose and the Camel Pose are some of the other things you can do to help yourself, and they can be quite beneficial.

The Vishuddha chakra is located close to the throat, and it is responsible for regulating the mouth, gums, and teeth as well as the trachea, thyroid, vertebrae, neck, throat, oesophagus, parathyroid, and hypothalamus. It has a direct impact on your feelings of safety, autonomy, self-expression, loyalty, communication, and organisation, as well as the ability to plan and organise.

The effects of having this chakra out of alignment can include having the flu, a fever, a sore throat, swollen glands, an imbalance in the thyroid, laryngitis, scoliosis, mouth ulcers, gum difficulties, vocal troubles, teeth problems, faith, criticism, addictions, and decision-making.

Your ability to communicate and your willpower are both centred in your throat chakra. This energy centre is to blame for any difficulties you have in selecting options or settling on a course of action. In addition to that, it acts as the centre of communication with a divine power. This spiritual power hub serves as the foundation for your faith. The throat chakra determines your ability to speak your mind and tell the truth to others. It also controls your ability to express your ideas. If you have a healthy throat chakra, you will be able to speak your truth without being inhibited by concerns about what other people will think or say. If, on the other hand, the chakra is blocked, it will cause anxiety about how other people will react to your viewpoints, which will ultimately lead to constraint.

Asanas de Yoga

Asanas, also known as yoga poses, are a fantastic tool for restoring harmony to our chakra system as well as cleaning it out. Stretching is good for our physical health in many ways. In addition, when it is combined with pranayama in yoga, it has the potential to put our chakras back into balance and give them new life (through oxygen).

While we are working on opening and balancing our chakras via the practise of chakra yoga, we will also be exposed to components of meditation that will help us improve our mental state. The following are some yoga positions that you can do to bring your chakras into balance and clear them out.

Chakra de l'origine

In light of the fact that this chakra is located at the base of the chakra system, you might want to think about including some of these positions into your routine.

the stance of a child

Forward bend from the head to the knees

Turns towards the front

Angle of recline on the bounds

The sacral chakra.

It is commonly referred to as the conduit for the fluidity that makes us human. Incorporate these positions into your regular yoga routine.

Pose de pigeon

Pose variations with open and bound angles

Doing the cow face pose

Chakra of the solar plexus.

Incorporate these poses into your practise to cultivate positive energy, to keep a controlled burn on your belly, and to facilitate direct transformation.

Do the boat pose

Assume a mountain pose

A salute to the sun

Leg raises

Chakra of the heart

The physical and spiritual dimensions of our lives are brought closer together through the practise of yoga with these postures.

The eagle stance

Performing backbends

Chakra of the Throat

These poses can be helpful in assisting us in purifying our inner selves and preserving an emotionally balanced state.

Do the camel pose

The bridge position

The plough pose

Pose in the shoulder stand

Chakra of the Third Eye

Through the practise of basic yoga postures, you can stimulate a positive flow of energy through your third eye chakra.

Pose like a cat or a cow

the stance of a child

Shoulder-stands (Shoulder-stands)

Chakra of the crown

Although meditation is considered to be an excellent exercise for the crown chakra, you can still use these poses to promote balance in the energy centres even though meditation is one of the best exercises for the crown chakra.

Position of death

Turns on the head

One lotus in half

Yoga of the Kundalini

The practise of chakra yoga is comparable to kundalini yoga, also called the yoga of awareness. The Western region was the first to receive it, all the way back in 1969. It combines the spiritual with the technical aspects of yoga so that the practitioner can achieve balance. It combines various postures with meditation on the breath in order to bring our chakra system into harmony.

The vital life force, also known as the Kundalini energy, can also be awoken with the help of the Kundalini technique. This energy is kept in our root chakra, which is located at the very base of our spine.

The goal of pranayama and poses in Kundalini yoga is to bring our physical bodies into a state of equilibrium. In addition to that, it integrates aspects of hatha yoga through a series of postures called kriyas. Kundalini is responsible for establishing the practise of using one's voice (such as chanting) in order to influence subtle positive changes in the body.

When we practise Kundalini yoga, we are primarily working towards the objective of directing energy from the base of our spine all the way to the crown of our heads. The method begins in the first chakra, awakening the Kundalini energy there. This energy then travels up the spine, activating the subsequent chakras in the progression. Once the energy reaches the seventh chakra, the cycle is considered to have come full circle. One finally reaches enlightenment.

Find Ways To Disconnect From Society And Reconnect With Yourself, And Good Luck With That!

You have to find ways that will enable you to disconnect from everything that is going on in the world around you. There are a lot of little things that you can do that will make it possible for you to disconnect and find the ideal equilibrium in the environment that you are in. Did you know that if you are able to remove the devices in your home that emit the noises that you hear in the night, you will be able to sleep more soundly? This is because the noises will no longer be coming from your home. Recent research has shown that the amount of white noise that is emitted by televisions and other electronic devices has recently made it extremely challenging for anyone to be able to sleep in a variety of settings. This issue has become increasingly prevalent in recent years. When you sleep, you ought to make sure that you are in a spot that is free from disturbances, both in terms of noise and physical obstacles. It is because your brain is unable to filter out many of the noises that you are experiencing while you are trying to rest that you have the impression that you are unable to rest. When there is a lot of noise and you are not in a good environment, your brain is unable to go into its deepest cycles of sleep and is unable to work its way through the cycles of sleep. Because of this, it is of the utmost significance to ensure that you are able to disconnect whenever necessary.

White Noise: When you are trying to concentrate on something and get something done, having white noise around you is often one of the worst things that can happen. Because of the level of noise, your brain may not be able to repair itself while you sleep, and this may mean that you will never be able to sleep in a way that will allow all of your cognitive function to be able to rest. When you go to bed at night, you should give some thought to turning off any sources of white noise. This includes turning off any electronic devices, such as radios and televisions, as well as turning off any cell phones that might be on. You should also consider sleeping in the complete darkness and making sure that all of the windows are covered in order to ensure that you are able to relax and repair while you are sleeping. This will allow you to sleep in a manner that will ensure you are able to sleep in a manner that will ensure you are able to sleep. Prepare to sleep in a room that is both cool and dry, and invest in the highest quality sheets you can find so that you can enjoy a restful night in conditions that are both cosy and refreshing. The best sheets to use for this purpose are ones made of linen or cotton that have the highest thread count available. That will make it possible for you to unwind and locate the ideal spot where you can genuinely escape from the day for a few minutes. After you have reclined yourself, you will have the opportunity to recuperate for a few minutes and give your body the chance to truly rest. Keep in mind that in order for your body to obtain the maximum amount of benefit from the healing process, it requires at least four uninterrupted hours of sleep. This indicates that when you lay your head down on the pillow, you should have at least four hours ahead of you, giving you the opportunity to complete at least one full cycle of sleep. The timing ensures that you will be able to reap all of the benefits of a restful night's sleep and that you will not feel exhausted the following day because you will have rested the night before. This is because you will have slept.

The amount of sleep that most of us get each night is causing a lot of problems in this day and age. It is not unheard of for a person to get fewer than three hours of sleep each night. When this occurs, the effect on the body is comparable to that which would occur if a person were to consume a significant amount of alcohol. This indicates that the individual must be content with the amount of sleep they get in order for the body and the mind to effectively repair themselves and for the individual to be able to relax. There is nothing more important than making sure that the person gets enough sleep so that they will be able to perform any job well and will also be able to concentrate, over the long term, on bettering their health. This will allow the person to be more productive.

After Having Gathered Your Energy In The Belly, You Will Now Send It To Various Chakra Areas.

The next step, which you should take after you have learned and mastered how to gather your breath, energy, or prana in your belly, is to distribute it to the other parts of your body.

This time, you will inhale and gather your breath or prana deep into the belly, and then as you exhale, you will direct it to other parts of the body that you are seeking to heal, and as you practise, you will imagine it happening.

If you are sick, injured, or otherwise unable to move freely, it is even more important for you to develop the skill of energy distribution. If you have a problem with your throat, for example, you can send the life force energy to your throat, and it won't be long before you start to notice changes in the way your throat feels. If you want to feel more compassion and love, direct your breath over your heart, then down your breastbone, and finally up your throat as you exhale. This will help you feel these emotions more.

Also, when any part of your body is stuck, such as your shoulders or hips, inhale the air deeply into your belly, and as you exhale, send energy or prana to the part of your body that is stuck. For example, inhale the air deeply into your belly when your shoulders or hips are stuck. You won't have to wait very long before you start to notice differences.

It may appear challenging to visualise how to keep your breath in your belly and send it as energy to different parts of your body, but with practise, it will become easier to do both of these things. When you practise breathing techniques to heal your chakra, one of the most important rules to keep in mind is that the energy and prana will follow the breath and the mind.

You can also help heal your prana by using the following breathing technique, which is broken down into steps.

Place yourself in a comfortable seated position, cross your legs, and make sure that your lips are gently sealed together while you breathe through your nose. Gather your palms into a prayer position and hold them aloft above your head.

Take in as much air as you can while focusing on inhaling all of it deeply into your stomach. You have the option of either squeezing them shut or opening them very wide. Imagine that you are able to absorb the maximum amount of light that is available to you as it travels through your eyes, the crown of your head, your face, and your ears.

When your lungs are completely expanded, prana will also fill them to capacity. Put your attention in the space between your eyes and then close your eyes, regardless of whether they were open or not. Create a point of focus in the space in between your eyebrows by forming a sphere of highly concentrated and bright light there. It is possible that you will see lightning flashes or sparks, but you must remember to keep your focus at all times, continue to focus, and keep yourself comfortable.

As you let out your breath, watch the light move to other areas of your body that need to be healed or brought back into balance. Repeat the exercise at least 10 or 15 times, or even more than that.

Our bodies are brimming with the vitality that we constantly inhale and exhale. In addition to coming from the air that we breathe, it also originates from the food that we eat, the water that we drink, and the sunlight that we expose ourselves to. The regular practise of these breathing techniques enables us to heal our chakras and make use of the vast amount of prana that resides within our bodies. In addition to this, our mental and spiritual selves, as well as our souls, are made whole. When we use these breathing techniques to help heal our chakras, we protect ourselves from experiencing any kind of physical discomfort or illness. We also give our lives meaning, coexist peacefully with others, make decisions that are in their best interests, and have wonderful connections with other people.

www.ingramcontent.com/pod-product-compliance
Lightning Source LLC
Chambersburg PA
CBHW052134110526
44591CB00012B/1719